FIT FOR THE KING

Sculpting Your Spiritual Muscles

PROPHETESS LENORE GILBERT

Dedication

The Lord gave the word; Great was the company of those who proclaimed it, Psalm 68:11 (NKJV)

Dedicated to my husband Aaron Gilbert, Jr

My Daughter Aaraven Gilbert

Charles and Candice Bailey

Eternal Heir Ministries

Metropolitan Services Inc

and

All those who support the Virtuous Woman Ministries

Your support, encouragement and belief is the motivating factor to finish this one of many more books to come, thank you all for your prayers and financial support

FIT FOR THE KING

PROPHETESS LENORE GILBERT

TABLE OF CONTENTS

ABOUT AUTHOR

Prophetess Lenore Gilbert is an accomplished author, community evangelist, and founder of Virtuous Woman Ministries in Nashville, Tennessee. With over two decades of experience as an entrepreneur and certified transformational coach, she has dedicated her life to helping people achieve spiritual fitness and apply the promises of God in practical ways to their lives and families. Through her book, "Fit for the King," Lenore aims to inspire and guide readers on their spiritual journey towards becoming fit for the King, Jesus Christ. As it is written in 1 Timothy 4:8 (KJV), "For bodily exercise profiteth little: but godliness is profitable unto all things, having promise of the life that now is, and of that which is to come."

INTRODUCTION

Dear Reader,

My name is Prophetess Lenore Gilbert, and I am so grateful that you have chosen to embark on this spiritual journey with me. As a community evangelist, founder of Virtuous Woman Ministries, and certified transformational coach, I have had the privilege of witnessing countless lives transformed through the power of God's love and grace. My hope is that this book, "Fit for the King," will inspire you to deepen your relationship with God and empower you to live a life full of purpose and passion.

In my own life, I have seen firsthand how God's promises, combined with a strong spiritual foundation, can make a world of difference. I have been blessed with a loving husband, Aaron Gilbert, Jr., and our beautiful daughter, Aaraven Gilbert, and my experiences as a wife and mother have only strengthened my belief in the importance of spiritual fitness.

"Fit for the King" is designed to be your guide on this journey towards spiritual fitness. In each chapter, we will explore essential aspects of a healthy and vibrant spiritual life, from understanding God's promises to cultivating faith, love, and forgiveness. Through practical tips and personal stories, you will learn how to overcome fear and doubt, establish a daily practice of prayer and meditation, and live your life with purpose, passion and fulfillment.

As you read through this book, I encourage you to reflect on your own life and consider the areas where you can deepen your relationship with God. Remember that spiritual fitness is not a destination but a continuous journey that requires commitment, dedication, and a willingness to grow. I hope that "Fit for the King" will serve as a valuable resource and companion on your path towards spiritual fitness, and that you will find inspiration, encouragement, and hope within these pages.

May God bless you as you embark on this journey, and may your life be a testament to the transformative power of God's love.

In His Service,

Prophetess Lenore Gilbert

Be Spiritually Fit...

As you journey through this book, take note of the moments that fill your heart with gratitude. Use the journal pages at the end of the book to record these precious memories, allowing you to reflect and meditate on how God has transformed your inner being.

Gratitude has the power to shift our perspective from self-pity to a profound appreciation of God's awe-inspiring splendor. Embrace this change, and let your heart of gratitude shine through.

CHAPTER 2
Understanding God's Promises

God's promises serve as a foundation for our faith and a source of hope and strength in our spiritual journey. They are the assurances that God has given to His people throughout the Bible, revealing His unwavering love, faithfulness, and commitment to our well-being. In this chapter, we will delve into the nature of these promises, explore their significance in our everyday lives, and learn how to claim them as our own.

The Nature of God's Promises

God's promises are more than just words; they are divine guarantees that reflect His character and nature. As we read the Bible, we encounter numerous promises that reveal God's love, provision, protection, and guidance. Some of the most well-known promises include eternal life for those who believe in Jesus Christ (John 3:16), peace that surpasses all understanding (Philippians 4:7), and the assurance that He will never leave us nor forsake us (Hebrews 13:5).

The Importance of God's Promises in Everyday Life

Understanding and embracing God's promises is essential for our spiritual growth and well-being. They provide us with hope during challenging times, assurance of God's presence in our lives, and a solid foundation for our faith. By holding onto these promises, we can experience comfort, strength, and peace even in the midst of trials and tribulations. The promises of God in Him are yes and in Him Amen, to the glory of God through us, His Glory works and lives through us, we are anointed in Christ and sealed by the Holy Spirit, this makes us fit as well as solid on a firm foundation in Jesus Christ. Living in the promises creates an atmosphere of expectancy in the present moment, in the present moment I expect something good and perfect from God, in the present moment I expect to not lean to my own understanding but lean into His promises, this causes an assurance in knowing that we are never alone, it takes spiritual fitness to believe by faith and not doubt., this is where we want to live and abide.

Identifying and Claiming God's Promises

To fully benefit from God's promises, we must learn to identify and claim them. Here are some practical steps to help you do so:

Study the Bible: Make a habit of reading the Bible regularly, as it is the primary source of God's promises. Take note of the passages that speak to your heart, and meditate on them. Pray them in your present moment, pray as though you have it.

Memorize Scriptures: Commit key verses that contain God's promises to memory. This will enable you to recall them quickly when you need encouragement or guidance.

Pray and Reflect: Ask God to reveal the promises that are specifically applicable to your life, and reflect on how they can shape your decisions, actions, and attitudes., and be willing to obey and receive the change.

Declare the Promises: Speak God's promises over your life, and declare them with confidence. This will help you internalize their truth and power, and enable you to stand firm in your faith.

Share with Others: Encourage fellow believers by sharing God's promises with them, and remind them of His faithfulness in times of need.

In conclusion, understanding God's promises is a vital aspect of our spiritual journey. By recognizing, claiming, and internalizing these divine assurances, we can build a strong foundation for our faith and experience the fullness of God's love, provision, and protection in our lives. As we continue to explore the various aspects of spiritual fitness, let us always remember that God's promises are the bedrock on which we stand. Upon this Rock I will build my church and the gates of hell shall not prevail against it Matt 16:18. Jesus is the Rock, our Rock, His promises are solid and ready for you to just say the promises and walk it out with power and authority.

CHAPTER 3
Prayer and Meditation

Prayer and meditation are essential practices in the life of a believer, as they provide a means to communicate with God and focus on His Word. Through these practices, we can deepen our relationship with God, gain insight into His will, and receive the strength and wisdom we need to navigate life's challenges. In this chapter, we will explore the importance of prayer and meditation, discuss practical tips for establishing a daily practice, and examine how these spiritual disciplines can transform our lives.

The Importance of Prayer and Meditation

Prayer is a powerful way to connect with God, express our gratitude and needs, and seek His guidance and intervention in our lives. The Bible encourages us to "pray without ceasing" (1 Thessalonians 5:17, KJV) and to "let your requests be made known unto God" (Philippians 4:6, KJV). Through prayer, we acknowledge our dependence on God and invite Him to work in our lives and circumstances.

Prayer brings healing, confess your trespasses to one another and pray for one another that you may be healed, the effectual fervent prayer of a righteous man avails much. James 5:16. Prayer and meditation are a spiritual muscle and it must be exercised daily and intentional, a desire, not a missed moment in prayer, this is important and will tone the attitude and bring all outside influence under subjection to the Lord.

Meditation, on the other hand, is the practice of focusing our thoughts on God's Word and reflecting on His truths. The psalmist wrote, "Blessed is the man that...meditates in [God's] law day and night" (Psalm 1:1-2, KJV). By meditating on Scripture, we internalize its teachings, deepen our understanding of God's character, and align our lives with His will.

Practical Tips for Establishing a Daily Practice

To develop a consistent habit of prayer and meditation, consider the following:

Set aside a specific time each day for prayer and meditation, ideally during a quiet and undisturbed period. Be ready and purposeful to meet the KING, go with expectancy.

Find a comfortable and peaceful place where you can focus on your conversation with God and reflection on His Word.

Use a Bible translation that resonates with you, such as the King James Version, and consider using a journal to record insights and prayers.

Begin your prayer time by expressing gratitude to God for His blessings and acknowledging His greatness (Psalm 100:4, KJV).

Be honest and open with God about your needs, concerns, and desires, remembering that He cares for you (1 Peter 5:7, KJV).

Meditate on specific passages of Scripture that address your current circumstances or spiritual needs, and reflect on their meaning and application in your life. Pray all prophetic words through and pray in the present moment of time, as though you have it.

How Prayer and Meditation Can Transform Your Life

When we consistently engage in prayer and meditation, we can experience profound transformation in various aspects of our lives:

Spiritual Growth: As we communicate with God and meditate on His Word, we grow in our understanding of His character and develop a deeper relationship with Him (James 4:8, KJV).

Renewed Mind: Meditation on Scripture helps renew our minds and align our thoughts with God's truth (Romans 12:2, KJV).

Peace and Comfort: In times of anxiety and distress, prayer and meditation can bring peace and comfort to our hearts, as promised in Philippians 4:6-7 (KJV).

Guidance and Wisdom: Seeking God's counsel through prayer and reflecting on His Word can provide us with the wisdom and direction we need to make sound decisions (Proverbs 3:5-6, KJV).

In conclusion, prayer and meditation are powerful spiritual practices that can transform our lives and deepen our relationship with God. By dedicating time each day to converse with God and meditate on His Word, we can experience spiritual growth, renewed minds, inner peace, and divine guidance. As we continue our journey towards spiritual fitness, let us remember the words of Jesus in Matthew 6:6 (KJV): "But thou, when thou prayest, enter into thy closet, and when thou hast shut thy door, pray to thy Father which is in secret; and thy Father which seeth in secret shall reward thee openly."

As we commit ourselves to consistent prayer and meditation, we can expect to see our lives transformed by the power of God's Word and the intimacy of our relationship with Him. These practices, in combination with the other aspects of spiritual fitness discussed throughout this book, will enable us to live lives that are truly "fit for the King." Let us always remember the value of these spiritual disciplines, and strive to make them a priority in our daily lives, as we grow closer to God and experience the richness of His love and grace.

CHAPTER 4
The Power of Faith

Faith is an essential component of the Christian life, serving as the foundation upon which our relationship with God is built. It is through faith that we believe in God's existence, trust in His promises, and experience His transformative power in our lives. In this chapter, we will explore the concept of faith, its importance in the Christian journey, and practical tips for strengthening our faith. We will also look at examples of how faith can help us overcome challenges and live a victorious life.

The Concept of Faith

Faith is defined in Hebrews 11:1 (KJV) as "the substance of things hoped for, the evidence of things not seen." In other words, faith is the assurance that what we hope for and believe in, though unseen, will come to pass because of God's faithfulness. Faith is not based on empirical evidence or human reasoning but on the unwavering trust in God and His Word. Now faith is the substance, substance is tangible, faith is present tense, faith is now.

The Importance of Faith in the Christian Life

Faith is crucial in the life of a believer for several reasons:

Salvation: It is through faith in Jesus Christ that we receive salvation and eternal life (Ephesians 2:8-9, KJV).

Relationship with God: Faith enables us to connect with God, as "without faith, it is impossible to please Him" (Hebrews 11:6, KJV).

Access to God's Promises: Our faith in God's Word allows us to claim His promises and experience their fulfillment in our lives (2 Corinthians 1:20, KJV).

Overcoming Challenges: Faith empowers us to overcome life's obstacles and emerge victorious (1 John 5:4, KJV).

Practical Tips for Strengthening Your Faith

To nurture and strengthen your faith, consider the following tips:

Study the Bible: Regularly reading and studying the Bible helps build a strong foundation for your faith, as "faith cometh by hearing, and hearing by the word of God" (Romans 10:17, KJV).

Pray: Prayer is essential for maintaining a close relationship with God, which in turn strengthens our faith (Mark 11:24, KJV).

Surround Yourself with Believers: Engaging with a community of believers encourages us to grow in our faith (Hebrews 10:25, KJV).

Put Your Faith into Action: Demonstrate your faith by serving others and obeying God's commandments (James 2:17, KJV).

Examples of Faith Overcoming Challenges

Throughout the Bible, we find inspiring examples of individuals who overcame challenges through faith:

Abraham: Despite his old age, Abraham believed in God's promise that he would become the father of many nations, and his faith was credited to him as righteousness (Genesis 15:6, KJV).

Moses: By faith, Moses led the Israelites out of Egypt and through the Red Sea, trusting in God's guidance and protection (Hebrews 11:27-29, KJV).

David: David's faith in God empowered him to defeat Goliath, the giant Philistine warrior, with a single stone and a sling (1 Samuel 17:45-47, KJV).

In conclusion, the power of faith is an essential element of the Christian life, enabling us to believe in God's promises, maintain a close relationship with Him, and overcome life's challenges. By actively nurturing and strengthening our faith through Bible study, prayer, fellowship, and acts of service, we can experience the transformative power of faith and live a victorious life. As we continue our journey towards spiritual growth and spiritual freedom, as believers we are raised up together and made to sit together in heavenly places in Christ Jesus, we have realms of access, these realms can only be accessed by faith.

CHAPTER 5
Overcoming Fear and Doubt

Fear and doubt are common experiences for many believers, often hindering our spiritual growth and preventing us from fully embracing God's promises. These feelings can arise from various sources, such as life's uncertainties, past failures, or negative influences from others. In this chapter, we will examine how fear and doubt can hold us back, discuss practical tips for overcoming these challenges, and share examples of people who have triumphed over fear and doubt to achieve great things in their spiritual journey.

The Impact of Fear and Doubt on Our Spiritual Lives

Fear and doubt can have a detrimental effect on our spiritual lives in several ways:

Weakened Faith: When we give in to fear and doubt, our faith in God and His promises can be weakened, hindering our relationship with Him (Matthew 14:31, KJV).

Paralysis: Fear and doubt can paralyze us, preventing us from taking necessary steps to grow in our faith and fulfill our God-given purpose (Matthew 25:25, KJV).

Missed Opportunities: By succumbing to fear and doubt, we may miss out on opportunities to serve God, experience His blessings, and impact the lives of others (Numbers 13:31-33, KJV).

Fear and doubt are barriers that create bondage, and leads one off of their path of destiny, God have given us a way of escape from fear and doubt, choose not to be fearful, choose not to doubt, these 2 spirits will keep us in opposition with God and all the promises He have for us. Get free from fear and doubt.

Practical Tips for Overcoming Fear and Doubt

To overcome fear and doubt in our spiritual lives, consider the following strategies:

Focus on God's Promises: Remind yourself of God's promises, as they can provide comfort and assurance in times of fear and doubt (Isaiah 41:10, KJV).

Pray for Strength: Pray for God's help in overcoming fear and doubt, trusting in His ability to provide the strength and courage you need (Philippians 4:13, KJV).

Surround Yourself with Supportive Believers: Engage with a community of believers who can encourage you, pray for you, and remind you of God's faithfulness (Proverbs 27:17, KJV).

Take Action: Despite your fears and doubts, take small steps of faith, trusting that God will be with you every step of the way (Joshua 1:9, KJV).

Examples of Overcoming Fear and Doubt

Throughout the Bible and in the lives of believers today, we see inspiring examples of individuals who overcame fear and doubt to achieve great things:

Peter: Despite initially sinking when he attempted to walk on water due to fear and doubt, Peter later became a bold apostle who fearlessly proclaimed the gospel (Matthew 14:29-31; Acts 4:13, KJV).

Gideon: Though initially fearful and doubtful of his ability to lead the Israelites against the Midianites, Gideon trusted in God's guidance and emerged victorious (Judges 6:15; 7:15-22, KJV).

Esther: Faced with the potential annihilation of her people, Esther overcame her fear and doubt to approach the king, ultimately saving the Jewish people from destruction (Esther 4:16; 5:1-2, KJV).

In conclusion, overcoming fear and doubt is an essential aspect of our spiritual journey, as it allows us to grow in faith, fulfill our God-given purpose, and experience God's blessings. By focusing on God's promises, praying for strength, surrounding ourselves with supportive believers, and taking action despite our fears, we can triumph over fear and doubt and become the powerful, faith-filled believers that God has called us to be. As we continue our journey towards spiritual fitness, let us always remember that "God hath not given us the spirit of fear ; but of power, and of love, and of a sound mind" (2 Timothy 1:7, KJV).

As we progress in our spiritual fitness journey, let us commit to facing and overcoming our fears and doubts, trusting in God's faithfulness and provision. By doing so, we can experience the abundant life that Jesus promised (John 10:10, KJV), and become more effective in fulfilling our God-given purpose.

Remember, fear and doubt are common human emotions, but with God's help, we can rise above them and live with confidence in His promises. As the Apostle Paul stated in Romans 8:31 (KJV), "If God be for us, who can be against us?" Keep this truth in your heart as you continue to grow spiritually, and know that with God on your side, you can overcome any fear or doubt that may arise in your life.

CHAPTER 6
Forgiveness and Love

Forgiveness and love are fundamental aspects of the Christian faith, rooted in the very nature of God and demonstrated by Jesus' sacrificial death on the cross. As believers, we are called to embody these virtues in our own lives, extending grace and love to others just as we have received them from God. In this chapter, we will explore the importance of forgiveness and love, discuss practical tips for cultivating these attributes in our lives, and share stories of people who have used forgiveness and love to heal relationships and transform their lives.

The Importance of Forgiveness and Love

Forgiveness and love are essential to our spiritual growth and overall well-being for several reasons:

Reflecting God's Character: By practicing forgiveness and love, we mirror the character of God, who has forgiven us of our sins and loves us unconditionally (Ephesians 4:32; 1 John 4:19, KJV).

Emotional Healing: Forgiveness frees us from the burden of resentment and bitterness, allowing for emotional healing and restoration (Colossians 3:13, KJV).

Strengthened Relationships: Forgiveness and love help mend broken relationships and promote unity among believers (1 Peter 4:8, KJV).

Spiritual Growth: Embracing forgiveness and love helps us grow spiritually, as we develop Christ-like qualities and become more like Him (2 Peter 3:18, KJV).

Practical Tips for Cultivating Forgiveness and Love

To foster forgiveness and love in your life, consider the following suggestions:

Reflect on God's Forgiveness: Regularly remind yourself of the forgiveness and grace that God has extended to you through Jesus' sacrifice on the cross (1 John 1:9, KJV).

Pray for a Forgiving Heart: Ask God to soften your heart and grant you the ability to forgive those who have hurt or wronged you (Matthew 6:12, KJV).

Seek Reconciliation: Whenever possible, take the initiative to seek reconciliation with those you need to forgive, striving to restore relationships and promote peace (Matthew 5:23-24, KJV).

Practice Loving Acts: Demonstrate love through acts of kindness, compassion, and service towards others, especially those who may be challenging to love (Luke 6:27-28, KJV).

Stories of Forgiveness and Love Transforming Lives

Throughout history and in the lives of believers today, we find inspiring examples of individuals whose lives have been transformed by forgiveness and love:

The Prodigal Son: In Jesus' parable of the prodigal son, the father's forgiveness and love for his wayward son led to the son's repentance and restoration, exemplifying God's grace and mercy towards us (Luke 15:11-32, KJV).

Joseph: Despite being sold into slavery by his brothers, Joseph forgave them and displayed love by providing for their needs during a famine, demonstrating the power of forgiveness to heal and restore relationships (Genesis 50:15-21, KJV)

Forgiveness and love are vital aspects of our spiritual journey, enabling us to reflect God's character, experience emotional healing, strengthen relationships, and grow spiritually. By cultivating these virtues through reflection, prayer, reconciliation, and loving acts, we can experience the transformative power of forgiveness and love in our own lives and the lives of those around us.

The Power of Forgiveness

Forgiveness is a transformative spiritual practice that enables us to release the burden of bitterness, resentment, and anger. By forgiving others and ourselves, we open our hearts to God's healing grace and experience a profound sense of freedom and inner peace.

Jesus Himself taught us the importance of forgiveness when He said, "For if you forgive other people when they sin against you, your heavenly Father will also forgive you" (Matthew 6:14, NIV). By practicing forgiveness, we not only follow Jesus's teachings but also allow ourselves to receive God's forgiveness and mercy.

The Importance of Love

Love is the foundation of our faith and the ultimate expression of our relationship with God. As the Apostle Paul reminds us, "And now these three remain: faith, hope, and love. But the greatest of these is love" (1 Corinthians 13:13, NIV). Love is the driving force behind all that we do as followers of Christ, guiding our actions and strengthening our connection with God and others.

Practical Tips for Embracing Forgiveness and Love

Practice Daily Forgiveness: Make a conscious effort to forgive those who have wronged you, even if the hurt runs deep. Pray for the strength and grace to let go of bitterness and resentment.

Forgive Yourself: Recognize that you, too, are deserving of forgiveness. Accept God's mercy and extend that same grace to yourself, releasing any guilt or self-condemnation.

Cultivate Empathy: Strive to understand the experiences and emotions of others. This empathy can help you foster forgiveness and deepen your capacity for love.

Love Unconditionally: Follow Jesus's example by loving others without judgment or conditions. Extend love and kindness to everyone, regardless of their background, beliefs, or actions.

Serve Others with Love: Seek opportunities to serve and care for those around you, demonstrating God's love through your actions.

As we strive to be Fit for the King (Jesus), let us remember the importance of forgiveness and love in our spiritual growth. By embracing these virtues, we open our hearts to God's transformative power, allowing Him to heal, restore, and strengthen our relationships with Him and with others. In doing so, we become a living testimony to the power of God's love and forgiveness in our lives.

CHAPTER 7
Gratitude and Praise

In this chapter, we will delve into the importance of gratitude and praise in our spiritual journey, and how cultivating an attitude of gratitude and praise can transform our lives. As we strive to be Fit for the King (Jesus), understanding and practicing gratitude and praise will help us grow closer to God and recognize His presence and blessings in our everyday lives.

Importance of Gratitude and Praise

Gratitude is the act of recognizing and appreciating the blessings in our lives, while praise is the expression of admiration and honor for God's grace, love, and protection. When we cultivate gratitude and praise, we open ourselves to the transformative power of God's love and develop a deep sense of contentment and happiness.

Gratitude and praise not only strengthen our relationship with God but also improve our mental and emotional well-being. Research has shown that practicing gratitude reduces stress, increases happiness, and improves our overall quality of life. Praise, on the other hand, brings us closer to God and helps us remain focused on His presence in our lives. Gratitude and praise creates an atmosphere of supernatural action to destroy the enemy and to create a confidence in accessing the promises of God

Practical Tips for Cultivating an Attitude of Gratitude and Praise

Keep a Gratitude Journal: Write down at least three things you are grateful for every day. This simple practice helps you develop an attitude of gratitude and recognize God's blessings in your life.

Practice Mindfulness: Take time every day to be present and fully engaged in your current activity. This can help you appreciate the beauty and blessings of each moment.

Share Your Gratitude: Express your gratitude to others by sharing your appreciation for their actions or their presence in your life. This not only fosters connection but also encourages others to develop gratitude.

Praise God Daily: Set aside time each day to praise God for His love, grace, and blessings. You can do this through prayer, worship, or simply by acknowledging His presence in your life.

Volunteer and Give Back: Serving others and giving back to your community can help you develop a deeper sense of gratitude and appreciation for the blessings you have received.

By cultivating an attitude of gratitude and praise, we open ourselves to the transformative power of God's love, allowing it to permeate every aspect of our lives. As we strive to be Fit for the King (Jesus), let us embrace these practices and grow closer to God, recognizing and appreciating His countless blessings in our lives and the lives of those around us.

Here are seven scriptures that focus on gratitude and praise:

Psalm 100:4
"Enter into his gates with thanksgiving, and into his courts with praise: be thankful unto him, and bless his name."

Colossians 3:15
"And let the peace of God rule in your hearts, to the which also ye are called in one body; and be ye thankful."

1 Thessalonians 5:18
"In every thing give thanks: for this is the will of God in Christ Jesus concerning you."

Psalm 107:8-9
"Oh that men would praise the LORD for his goodness, and for his wonderful works to the children of men! For he satisfieth the longing soul, and filleth the hungry soul with goodness."

Hebrews 13:15
"By him therefore let us offer the sacrifice of praise to God continually, that is, the fruit of our lips giving thanks to his name."

Psalm 150:6
"Let everything that hath breath praise the LORD. Praise ye the LORD."

Psalm 28:7
"The LORD is my strength and my shield; my heart trusted in him, and I am helped: therefore my heart greatly rejoiceth; and with my song will I praise him."

CHAPTER 8
Spiritual Fitness Training

In this chapter, we will explore the concept of spiritual fitness and its importance in our journey to be Fit for the King (Jesus). We will also provide practical tips for staying spiritually fit and discuss examples of how spiritual fitness can improve your life.

Explanation of Spiritual Fitness and Why It's Important

Spiritual fitness refers to the development and maintenance of a strong, healthy, and vibrant relationship with God. It involves nurturing our spirit through prayer, meditation, worship, and the study of God's Word. Spiritual fitness is vital for our overall well-being, as it helps us connect with our true purpose and align our actions with God's will.

A spiritually fit person is better equipped to handle life's challenges, find inner peace, and experience lasting joy. Spiritual fitness strengthens our faith, enables us to grow closer to God, and empowers us to share His love with others.

Practical Tips for Staying Spiritually Fit

Develop a Daily Prayer Routine: Set aside time each day for prayer and make it a non-negotiable part of your schedule. Regular communication with God helps strengthen your relationship with Him and maintain spiritual fitness.

Study the Bible: Make a habit of reading and studying the Bible daily. God's Word is a powerful tool for personal growth, guidance, and spiritual nourishment.

Attend Church and Fellowship: Regularly attend church services and engage in fellowship with other believers. Being part of a faith community can provide support, encouragement, and accountability for your spiritual growth.

Practice Spiritual Disciplines: Engage in spiritual disciplines such as fasting, meditation, and silence. These practices can deepen your connection with God and enhance your spiritual fitness.

Serve Others: Look for opportunities to serve others in your community and beyond. Acts of service demonstrate God's love and help you develop a servant's heart.

Share Your Faith: Share your faith with others, both through your words and actions. This not only strengthens your own spiritual fitness but also encourages others in their spiritual journey.

Examples of How Spiritual Fitness Can Improve Your Life

Enhanced Resilience: Spiritual fitness can help you develop the ability to bounce back from challenges and difficulties, trusting in God's plan and His strength to guide you through tough times.

Improved Relationships: When you prioritize spiritual fitness, your relationships with others can also improve, as you become more patient, understanding, and loving.

Greater Sense of Purpose: Spiritual fitness can help you discover and embrace your God-given purpose in life, leading to a more fulfilling and meaningful existence.

Increased Inner Peace: As you grow spiritually fit, you can experience increased inner peace and contentment, even in the midst of life's storms.

Empowerment to Make Positive Changes: Spiritual fitness can provide you with the strength and courage needed to make positive changes in your life, such as breaking unhealthy habits or pursuing new opportunities.

By prioritizing spiritual fitness, you can experience a deeper connection with God, grow in your faith, and enjoy a more abundant and fulfilling life. As you strive to be Fit for the King (Jesus), make spiritual fitness an essential component of your daily routine and watch the transformation it brings to every aspect of your life.

CHAPTER 9
Living with Purpose and Passion

In this chapter, we will delve into the importance of living with purpose and passion, providing practical tips for discovering your purpose and embracing a passionate life. We will also share examples of individuals who have found their purpose and are living with passion, inspiring us to strive for a meaningful and fulfilling existence.

Importance of Living with Purpose and Passion

Living with purpose and passion is vital for our overall well-being and spiritual growth. When we discover our God-given purpose and pursue it with passion, we experience a deep sense of fulfillment, contentment, and joy. Embracing our purpose enables us to align our actions with God's plan for our lives, make a positive impact on the world, and grow closer to Him.

A life filled with purpose and passion not only brings personal satisfaction but also glorifies God by demonstrating His love, grace, and transformative power in our lives.

Practical Tips for Discovering Your Purpose and Living with Passion

Pray for Guidance: Ask God to reveal His purpose for your life. Be open to His guidance and trust that He will lead you to your purpose in His perfect timing.

Assess Your Strengths and Gifts: Reflect on your natural talents, skills, and passions. Consider how these can be used to serve God and others, ultimately contributing to your purpose.

Seek Wise Counsel: Consult with trusted spiritual mentors, friends, or family members who can provide valuable insights and guidance as you search for your purpose.

Take Action: Begin taking steps toward your purpose, even if you're not entirely certain what it is yet. As you move forward, your path may become clearer, and your passion may grow stronger.

Stay Committed: Embrace your purpose with determination, and be prepared to face challenges along the way. Trust in God's strength to help you persevere and maintain your passion.

By discovering and embracing our purpose, we can live with passion and experience the abundant life God has planned for us. As we strive to be Fit for the King (Jesus), let us commit to pursuing our God-given purpose with unwavering passion, trusting that He will use us to make a difference in the world and bring glory to His name.

CHAPTER 10
Spiritual Fitness

As we reach the conclusion of this spiritual journey, I, Prophetess Lenore Gilbert, encourage you to reflect on the powerful lessons and insights we have explored in this book. Our goal has been to help you become Fit for the King (Jesus) by nurturing your spiritual growth, embracing God's promises, and applying them in your everyday life.

As you continue on your path to spiritual fitness, remember that the key to a thriving and fulfilling relationship with God lies in your commitment, perseverance, and openness to His guidance. Embrace the transformative power of gratitude, praise, and living with purpose and passion. Trust that as you grow spiritually fit, you will experience the abundant life that God has in store for you and your loved ones.

To further strengthen your spiritual journey, I exhort you to:

Stay Connected to God: Remain steadfast in prayer, Bible study, and worship. These practices will help you maintain a close relationship with God and deepen your understanding of His will for your life.

Stay Accountable: Surround yourself with like-minded believers who can support, encourage, and hold you accountable as you strive for spiritual growth.

Stay Teachable: Be open to God's wisdom and guidance, even when it challenges your preconceived ideas or beliefs. Remember that spiritual growth requires humility and a willingness to learn.

Stay Focused on the Eternal: Keep your eyes on the eternal promises of God, rather than getting caught up in the fleeting distractions of this world. This focus will provide you with the strength and determination needed to persevere in your spiritual journey.

Stay Committed to Service: Look for opportunities to serve others and demonstrate God's love in your community. Acts of service not only bring joy and fulfillment but also help you grow closer to God and the people around you.

As you embark on this journey toward spiritual fitness, know that you are never alone. God is with you every step of the way, providing guidance, strength, and love. Trust in His divine plan for your life and be prepared to embrace the growth and transformation that await you.

May the Lord bless and keep you as you strive to be Fit for the King (Jesus). May your heart be filled with gratitude, your spirit be nourished with His Word, and your life be a testament to His love, grace, and power.

Gratitude brings change to our attitude

Gratitude brings change to our attitude, having a heart of gratitude reflects on those moments when we decide to change our mind from a place of self pity to a place of God's awesome splendor. The enemy hates a grateful heart, when one has a grateful heart they will begin to see their life on a better spectrum, I would like to say with rose colored glasses, look at where you are now in the present moment and realize you are better now in Christ than you were before. Every dark place being grateful sheds light on those dark areas and your current situation will always change for the better.

Steps to being grateful, look back over your life, and see where you are now, and give God a huge shout out, start expressing to others all God have done for you and continuing to do for you, even when you don't fully understand outcomes that may not be in your favor, be exceedingly glad, this type of grateful expression confuse the enemy and it pleases God because your gratitude brings you to a level of trusting God for the journey even though it may be uncomfortable.

Just smile, when people smile it changes the whole mood of an individual, most smiles bring and promote gratefulness. Think of others, start thinking about positive people, inspiring people God have placed into your life, these individuals are called destiny helpers, always think and reach out to your destiny helpers, for these are important people God strategically placed in your life for growth in Jesus , growth within yourself as your help others on your journey.

Bless everything God has given you, bless your food, bless your job and others on your job, bless your home, your car, bless your family, bless your friends, words of blessing to others will allow you to be grateful for all the things He has given you, even bless your vitamins, and medications.

In His Service,
Prophetess Lenore Gilbert
Founder, Virtuous Woman Ministries Nashville, TN
Use the following journal pages to express thankfulness for His many blessings and record the moments when you've witnessed His love and grace. In times of doubt or struggle, revisit these pages to remind yourself of God's unwavering faithfulness.

Today I'm grateful for...

_____

_____

_____

_____

_____

_____

_____

_____

_____

_____

_____

Today I'm grateful for...

_____

_____

_____

_____

_____

_____

_____

_____

_____

_____

_____

_____

_____

_____

Today I'm grateful for...

_____

_____

_____

_____

_____

_____

_____

_____

_____

_____

_____

_____

Today I'm grateful for...

_____

_____

_____

———————————————————————

———————————————————————

———————————————————————

———————————————————————

———————————————————————

———————————————————————

———————————————————————

———————————————————————

———————————————————————

———————————————————————

Today I'm grateful for...

———————————————————————

———————————————————————

———————————————————————

———————————————————————

———————————————————————

_____

_____

_____

_____

_____

_____

_____

_____

Today I'm grateful for...

_____

_____

_____

_____

_____

_____

_____

_____

_____

_____

_____

_____

_____

Today I'm grateful for...

_____

_____

_____

_____

_____

_____

_____

_____

_____

_____

_____

_____

_____

Today I'm grateful for...

_____

_____

_____

_____

_____

_____

_____

_____

_____

_____

_____

_____

_____

_____

Today I'm grateful for...

_____

_____

_____

_____

_____

_____

_____

_____

_____

_____

_____

_____

_____

_____

Today I'm grateful for...

_____

_____

_____

_____

_____

_____

_____

_____

_____

_____

_____

_____

_____

Today I'm grateful for...

_____

_____

_____

_____

_____

_____

_____

_____

_____

_____

_____

_____

_____

Today I'm grateful for...

Today I'm grateful for...

_____

_____

_____

_____

_____

_____

_____

_____

_____

_____

_____

_____

Today I'm grateful for...

_____

_____

_____

_____

_____

_____

_____

_____

_____

_____

_____

_____

_____

Today I'm grateful for...

_____

_____

_____

_____

_____

_____

_____

_____

_____

_____

_____

_____

_____

_____

Today I'm grateful for...

_____

_____

_____

LENORE GILBERT

_____

_____

_____

_____

_____

_____

_____

_____

_____

_____

Today I'm grateful for...

_____

_____

_____

_____

_____

Today I'm grateful for...

LENORE GILBERT

_____

_____

_____

_____

_____

_____

_____

Today I'm grateful for...

_____

_____

_____

_____

_____

_____

_____

_____

_____

_____

_____

_____

_____

Today I'm grateful for...

_____

_____

_____

_____

_____

_____

_____

_____

_____

_____

_____

_____

_____

_____

_____

May these powerful scriptures serve as a source of inspiration and encouragement as you reflect on your own experiences of gratitude:

1 Thessalonians 5:18 (KJV):

"In every thing give thanks: for this is the will of God in Christ Jesus concerning you."

Psalm 107:1 (KJV):

"O give thanks unto the LORD, for he is good: for his mercy endureth for ever."

Dear Friends,

I am Lenore Gilbert, the author of "Fit For The King - Sculpting Your Spiritual Muscles", and the founder of Virtuous Woman Ministries. Our mission at Virtuous Woman Ministries is to empower women to grow spiritually and live victorious lives in Christ.

We offer a range of resources and tools to help women cultivate their spiritual lives, including online courses, devotionals, coaching programs and conferences. Our community of women is dedicated to supporting and encouraging one another on this journey of faith.

If you haven't already, I encourage you to visit our website at www.VirtuousWomanMinistries.org and sign up for our newsletter. By doing so, you'll gain access to exclusive content and be the first to know about our upcoming events and programs.

Together, let's continue to grow in our relationship with Christ and live out our calling as virtuous women!

Blessings, Prophetess Lenore Gilbert

Call or Text
(615) 596-1150
(470) 588-7093

Made in the USA
Columbia, SC
15 December 2024

49162900R00036